Family Devotions Based on Christmas Carols

Christ-Centered Advent

Hal & Melanie Young

GREAT WATERS PRESS
MAKING BIBLICAL FAMILY LIFE PRACTICAL

©2020 Hal & Melanie Young, All Rights Reserved
Great Waters Press

www.RaisingRealMen.com

If purchased in eBook format, this eBook is not licensed for resale. This license is personal to the original purchaser and may not be sold, loaned, or otherwise transferred to third parties or additional users. Purchaser may make one copy for each member of their immediate household. Additional Licenses should be purchased if you'd like to share this eBook with anyone outside your family. Unlimited copies may be made only of pages containing words of Christmas Carols for singing. Contact info@greatwaterspress.com for information.

Copying for school or co-op use is strictly prohibited. Each student should purchase their own copy.

No part of this publication may otherwise be published, reproduced, stored in a retrieval system, or transmitted or copied in any form or by any means now known or hereafter developed, whether electronic, mechanical, or otherwise, without prior written permission of the publisher. Illegal use, copying, publication, transfer or distribution is considered copyright infringement according to Sections 107 and 108 and other relevant portions of the United States Copyright Act.

The use of any trademarked names does not imply endorsement or approval by the companies holding those trademarks. This document is intended only to enhance your user experience.

All interior fine art illustrations are in the public domain.

Cover Design, Melanie Young, Copyright © 2020, All rights reserved.

Cover Art, Susannah Ruth Young, Copyright © 2020, All rights reserved.

Scripture taken from either the New King James Version or the English Standard Version.

New King James Version, Copyright © 1982 by Thomas Nelson, Inc. Used by permission. All rights reserved,

English Standard Version, copyright © 2001 by Crossway Bibles, a publishing ministry of Good News Publishers. Used by permission. All rights reserved.

Contents

Before You Begin 4

Week One

The Christmas Carols 5

O Come All Ye Faithful 6

    O Come Let Us Adore Him 10

    God of God, Light of Light 13

    Sing, Choirs of Angels 18

    Born This Happy Morning 20

Week Two

Hark, the Herald Angels Sing 22

    Veiled in Flesh, the Godhead See 26

    Born That Man No More May Die 28

    Come, Desire of Nations, Come 31

    A Day of Mercy 34

Week Three

We Three Kings of Orient Are 35

    Born a King on Bethlehem's Plain 39

    Worshipping God on High 41

    Sealed in the Stone Cold Tomb 43

    Glorious Now Behold Him Arise 45

Week Four

Angels from the Realms of Glory 47

    Brighter Visions Beam Afar 51

    Watching Long in Hope and Fear 53

    Mercy Calls You 56

    All Creation, Join in Praising 58

BEFORE YOU BEGIN

For many years, we've taught our children the hymns of the faith through what we call the Hymn of the Week. Each day we sing all the verses of the song we're learning and explain one of the verses. By the end of the week, even the young children have learned to sing the hymn and understand it. We can sing for hours in the van without a hymnbook – such a blessing!

This has been particularly precious to us during the Christmas season. Christmas hymns or carols are so full of rich theology that it's a shame to just sing the first verse, which is usually the introduction, and never even consider the rest.

Christians have been celebrating the birth of Christ in song since the 3rd or 4th century. *O Come, O Come Emmanuel* was written twelve hundred years ago! The tradition of caroling, walking from house to house singing Christmas carols, dates back to at least the 13th century.

In this Christmas devotional, we use that ancient tradition and the dear hymns of the Advent season, the time when we anticipate celebrating the Incarnation, when the Word was made flesh, and the birth of Christ, to point our children to the gospel and encourage us all to worship.

Come and join us.

Choose a time when you can all gather for a few minutes. We like to open in prayer. Don't make it too complicated, just ask the Lord to help you all to understand what is being taught and to teach you to love and trust Him.

Sing the entire carol, all the verses, every weekday. We've provided four weeks of devotions with four or five lessons per week.

After you sing, explain the verse for that day. Don't worry if it seems you're your children's heads. We've been shocked by how much kids can grasp if you give them a chance. Answer any questions and talk about what it means for your lives. Close in prayer, praying about the requests any of you have. It should take about 15 minutes a day. If you keep it short and doable, you won't have as much trouble doing it consistently!

Enjoy!

Week 1, Day 1
The Christmas Carols

For the next few weeks, we are going to be using Christmas carols as the basis for our devotions! Let's read what the Bible says about singing:

Look carefully then how you walk, not as unwise but as wise, making the best use of the time, because the days are evil. Therefore do not be foolish, but understand what the will of the Lord is. And do not get drunk with wine, for that is debauchery, but be filled with the Spirit, addressing one another in psalms and hymns and spiritual songs, singing and making melody to the Lord with your heart, giving thanks always and for everything to God the Father in the name of our Lord Jesus Christ, submitting to one another out of reverence for Christ. Ephesians 5:15-21

Singing songs of praise to God is something we should be doing whether anyone is listening or not, "singing and making melody to the Lord with your heart..." because it one of the ways that God tells us to worship Him.

We should also be singing with others, though. The passage says, "addressing one another in psalms and hymns and spiritual songs." That's why we sing in church and why it's a good idea for us to sing as a family.

There is a lot to be learned from singing the songs of the faith. Here's a passage that makes that clear:

Let the word of Christ dwell in you richly, teaching and admonishing one another in all wisdom, singing psalms and hymns and spiritual songs, with thankfulness in your hearts to God. Colossians 3:16

Singing hymns can be part of letting the word of Christ dwell in us and part of teaching and admonishing (that means to warn or advise) one another, too.

That's what we are going to be doing – learning the Christmas carols, but also learning about what they mean and what they can teach us about Jesus.

O Come All Ye Faithful
Adeste Fideles

Adoration of the Magi, Rubens, 1617-18

"O Come All Ye Faithful" is the English translation of the Latin hymn "Adestes Fideles." There is a great deal of dispute as to who wrote it. A variety of authors have been proposed, from St. Bonaventure in the 13th Century to King John IV, the Musician King, of Portugal, when his daughter Catherine traveled to England to marry King Charles II. One likely author and probable composer is John Francis Wade, who first published the hymn text and tune together in his *Cantus Diversi* in 1751. Whole academic dissertations have been written on the origin of this hymn.

Did you know one verse is taken almost exactly from an ancient creed? We'll also be learning about angels and who is called the Word. Today, let's just sing it.

[Play a midi file with the tune <u>at Hymnary</u> where you can also read more about it.]

O Come All Ye Faithful

The words of the second verse are directly from one of the oldest creeds.

O come, all ye faithful, joyful and triumphant,
O come ye, O come ye, to Bethlehem.
Come and behold Him, born the King of angels;

Refrain

O come, let us adore Him,
O come, let us adore Him,
O come, let us adore Him,
Christ the Lord.

God of God, Light of Lights,
Lo, He abhors not the Virgin's womb;
Son of the Father, begotten, not created;

Refrain

Sing, choirs of angels, sing in exultation;
O sing, all ye citizens of heaven above!
Glory to God, all glory in the highest;

Refrain

Yea, Lord, we greet Thee, born this happy morning;
Jesus, to Thee be glory given;
Word of the Father, now in flesh appearing.

Refrain

Adestes Fideles

If you are studying Latin with your children, or plan to, or if your children just enjoy history or languages, they may really enjoy singing the original Latin words.

Adeste fideles læti triumphantes,
Venite, venite in Bethlehem.
Natum videte, Regem angelorum:

Refrain
Veníte adoremus,
Veníte adoremus
Veníte adoremus Dóminum

Deum de Deo, lumen de lumine
Gestant puellæ viscera
Deum verum, genitum non factum.

Refrain

Cantet nunc io, chorus angelorum;
Cantet nunc aula cælestium,
Gloria, gloria in excelsis Deo,

Refrain

Ergo qui natus die hodierna.
Jesu, tibi sit gloria,
Patris æterni Verbum caro factum.

Refrain

O Come All Ye Faithful
Additional Verses

There are four additional verses written by a Catholic priest in the mid-1800s. Our family had never heard these before this year, but our son, who studied at Oxford, tells us they are much more common in England and Europe. We won't be discussing these, but we are including them for your interest or if they are favorites you would like to sing.

See how the shepherds, summoned to His cradle,
Leaving their flocks, draw nigh to gaze;
We too will thither bend our joyful footsteps;

Refrain

Lo! Star led chieftains, Magi, Christ adoring,
Offer Him incense, gold, and myrrh;
We to the Christ Child bring our hearts' oblations.

Refrain

Child, for us sinners poor and in the manger,
We would embrace Thee, with love and awe;
Who would not love Thee, loving us so dearly?

Refrain

Week 1, Day 2
O Come Let Us Adore Him

The Adoration of the Magi, Botticelli, 1475

Let's sing O Come All Ye Faithful again. Now, let's learn more about it!

The first verse of this lovely hymn calls the faithful to Bethlehem to behold the newborn King. Why are they joyful and triumphant? Because at last their Messiah is come to conquer sin and death!

O come, all ye faithful, joyful and triumphant,
O come ye, O come ye, to Bethlehem.

Come and behold Him, born the King of angels;

Refrain (Also known as the chorus, this is the part we repeat after every verse.)

O come, let us adore Him,
O come, let us adore Him,
O come, let us adore Him,
Christ the Lord.

"Come to Bethlehem," is an invitation full of meaning because more than 500 years before Christ's birth, the prophet Micah announced:

But you, Bethlehem Ephrathah, Though you are little among the thousands of Judah, Yet out of you shall come forth to Me The One to be Ruler in Israel, Whose goings forth are from of old, From everlasting. Micah 5:2

Bethlehem was the chosen birthplace of the King of Israel who was from old, from everlasting. In other words, the eternal God! It is amazing to think that the Lord would lead Caesar Augustus in far away Rome to call for a census at the perfect time to require Joseph and Mary to be in Bethlehem the very day the Christ Child was to be born. Read Luke 2:1-6:

In those days a decree went out from Caesar Augustus that all the world should be registered. This was the first registration when Quirinius was governor of Syria. And all went to be registered, each to his own town. And Joseph also went up from Galilee, from the town of Nazareth, to Judea, to the city of David, which is called Bethlehem, because he was of the house and lineage of David, to be registered with Mary, his betrothed, who was with child. And while they were there, the time came for her to give birth.

We serve a mighty and sovereign God, who holds the heart of the king in his hand to do with it what He will, as it says in Proverbs 21:1.

What does it mean to adore Him? The word adore means to worship as God. Kind of makes you wonder why we find ourselves saying we "adore chocolate" or "adore kittens." The meaning of words does change over the years and adorable now means cute and loveable, but adore in this refrain definitely means to worship, to lovingly honor and respect.

Before we close, I'd like to say a few words about the artwork we chose to go with this verse. It's the "Adoration of the Magi", which means the worship of the wise men, and it was painted by Sandro Botticelli, an Italian Renaissance master, in 1475. Do you notice that many of the magi are dressed in Renaissance style clothing? Many artists dressed Biblical characters in their own fashion (and ethnicity!), not out of ignorance, but in an effort to help people see themselves in the story. In fact, several of the characters seen in this painting were modeled on individuals in the Medici family, rulers of Florence, where Botticelli worked.

Next, notice the crumbling columns in the background. We have a reproduction of an Old Master in our house that shows the Christ Child and lamb on Classical ruins. Interest in the Classical time period revived in the Renaissance, so they were very interested in those subjects, but I have often wondered if the artists were showing the Classical civilizations of Rome and Greece crumbing under their sin, while Christ comes to the fore. This painting is currently held in the Uffizi Gallery in Florence and our son Caleb was able to visit there. I wonder if he saw this masterpiece? Can you imagine a painting showing our country's leaders worshiping the Christ child? What about our family? The Bible tells us in Romans 14:11,

for it is written,
"As I live, says the Lord, every knee shall bow to me,
and every tongue shall confess to God."

So, one day everyone will confess that Jesus is Lord. It's a lot better to do that now, though. Let's pray. What do we need to pray about today?

Week 1, Day 3
God of God, Light of Light

The Virgin and Child Embracing, Sassoferrato, 1660-85

Today's lesson is a little longer, but it's really interesting! Have you ever repeated a creed in church? Many of us have at least heard The Apostle's Creed before, "I believe in God the Father, Maker of Heaven and Earth," is how it begins. A creed is a statement of belief. It comes from the Latin word *credo*, which means, "I believe".

Why do churches use creeds?

In the early years of the church, just like today, the church was plagued by those who wanted to twist the truth of God's Word to advance their own agenda. The Council of Nicea, a meeting of Christian leaders from all over the known world, was confronted by one of these heresies at their meeting in the year 325. The Arian heresy, named after Arius, one of the men teaching it, had been spreading through many churches. The Arians taught that Jesus Christ was not God, but merely a created being.

Why do we call that a heresy? A heresy is an untruth, or lie, taught about God and His Word. We know that the Arians were teaching heresy because their doctrine is contradicted by the Word of God. John 1 teaches:

In the beginning was the Word, and the Word was with God, and the Word was God. He was in the beginning with God. All things were made through him, and without him was not any thing made that was made. In him was life, and the life was the light of men. The light shines in the darkness, and the darkness has not overcome it.

There was a man sent from God, whose name was John. He came as a witness, to bear witness about the light, that all might believe through him. He was not the light, but came to bear witness about the light.

The true light, which gives light to everyone, was coming into the world. He was in the world, and the world was made through him, yet the world did not know him. He came to his own, and his own people did not receive him. But to all who did receive him, who believed in his name, he gave the right to become children of God, who were born, not of blood nor of the will of the flesh nor of the will of man, but of God.

And the Word became flesh and dwelt among us, and we have seen his glory, glory as of the only Son from the Father, full of grace and truth. John 1:1-14

The Council decided that it was important for real Christians to have a statement that they could all agree on, setting forth the essentials of the faith. That statement, as edited by subsequent church councils, became the Nicene Creed, and it is not only one of the most ancient creeds, or doctrinal statements, but it is the only one used frequently in Protestant, Orthodox *and* Roman Catholic assemblies.

The second verse of "O Come All Ye Faithful" is taken from the Nicene Creed. In fact, the Latin is taken word for word from the creed. Here's the creed, translated into English:

I believe in one God,
the Father Almighty,
maker of heaven and earth,
and of all things visible and invisible;

And in one Lord Jesus Christ,
the only begotten Son of God,
begotten of his Father before all worlds,
God of God, Light of Light,
very God of very God,
begotten, not made,
being of one substance with the Father;
by whom all things were made;
who for us men and for our salvation
came down from heaven,
and was incarnate by the Holy Ghost
of the Virgin Mary,
and was made man;
and was crucified also for us under Pontius Pilate;
he suffered and was buried;
and the third day he rose again
according to the Scriptures,
and ascended into heaven,
and sitteth on the right hand of the Father;
and he shall come again, with glory,
to judge both the quick and the dead;
whose kingdom shall have no end.

And I believe in the Holy Ghost the Lord, and Giver of Life,
who proceedeth from the Father [and the Son];
who with the Father and the Son together
is worshipped and glorified;
who spake by the Prophets.
And I believe one holy catholic and apostolic Church;
I acknowledge one baptism for the remission of sins;
and I look for the resurrection of the dead,
and the life of the world to come. AMEN.

Catholic, in this creed, is a word meaning universal, all Christians everywhere.

And now, let's look at the stanza for today:

God of God, Light of Light,
Lo, He abhors not the Virgin's womb;
Son of the Father, begotten, not created;

If you're wondering how in the world to sing the first line, it's like this: God uh-of Go-od, Li-ight uh-of Li-ights.

Do you see where in the creed the different phrases come from? Can you find several of those same phrases in John 1? This is a direct counter to the Arian heresy: Jesus *is* God of God – the same substance as God the Father. Light of light was a favorite explanation of the co-existence of God the Father and God the Son used by Athanasius, the chief defender of the truth at the council. Many times in Scripture light is used to describe Jesus, such as in Isaiah 9:2 and Isaiah 60:1-3.

Also, Jesus is the Son of the Father, begotten, not created. Jesus is *not* a part of the creation but is, instead, the Creator. It makes all the difference in the world. A mere man could not have died for any sins but his own; only a sinless, infinite God could have died for the sins of many.

The most questions people have about this verse come from the second line, where it says "He abhors not the virgin's womb," but it is quite understandable when you know church history. Even before the Arians, there was the gnostic heresy which taught that the material world, all matter, is evil and that as a pure spirit, God would abhor becoming flesh. They did not believe that Jesus was a material being at all, but only *appeared* to come in the flesh. Just as the Arians denied Christ was God, the Gnostics denied that He was man. If He had not come in the flesh, He could not have lived a holy life and died for our sins. The Gnostics teach that man is saved by special knowledge that enables him to gradually leave the material body and become pure spirit. That is not Christianity; it is a false gospel.

Why are we going into all this ancient Church history? **Because these heresies are alive and well.** If you think about it, you can probably identify three or four major cults that teach one of these heresies. Every cult denies at least one of these very essentials of the faith: Christ is God come in the flesh, both God and man, and salvation is by faith in Christ's substitutionary death alone, not by works or knowledge. It's essential to know the truth of God and to point out the problems in the counterfeits that Satan will put in our paths.

Enjoy singing the words that Christians have been saying to affirm the essentials of the faith for nearly 1700 years!

Let's pray!

Week 1, Day 4
Sing, Choirs of Angels

The Angel Appearing to the Shepherds, etching, Rembrandt, 1634

Sing, choirs of angels, sing in exultation;
O sing, all ye citizens of heaven above!
Glory to God, all glory in the highest;

Angels are God's messengers, and they appear all through the story of Christ's birth. The angel Gabriel explained God's plan for Jesus' birth to Mary (Luke 1:26-38) and then to Joseph (Matthew 1:18-25), and later an unnamed angel warned Joseph to take Jesus and Mary to Egypt for His safety (Matthew 2:13-15). The most famous appearance, though, is a **multitude** of them who appeared to shepherds:

Now there were in the same country shepherds living out in the fields, keeping watch over their flock by night. And behold, an angel of the Lord stood before them, and the glory of the Lord shone around them, and they were greatly afraid. Then the angel said to them, "Do not be afraid, for behold, I bring you good tidings of great joy which will be to all people. For there is born to you this day in the city of David a Savior, who is Christ the Lord. And this will be the sign to you: You will find a Babe wrapped in swaddling cloths, lying in a manger."

And suddenly there was with the angel a multitude of the heavenly host praising God and saying:

*"Glory to God in the highest,
And on earth peace, goodwill toward men!"* Luke 2:8-14

So, in this verse, we aren't just surprised like the shepherds were — we're cheering the angels on! **"Sing, choirs of angels! Sing in exaltation!"**

And while the verse speaks of angels, we can also remember that believers here on earth are also **"citizens of heaven above."** Paul says that we believers are:

no longer strangers and foreigners, but fellow citizens with the saints and members of the household of God... Ephesians 2:19

For our citizenship is in heaven, from which we also eagerly wait for the Savior, the Lord Jesus Christ. Philippians 3:20

This Christmas, we can raise our voices and join with the angels' voices, to praise the newborn and everlasting King!

Tip for Singing: Remember that Paul said we are "speaking and admonishing one another" with our songs. Our words should make sense! Sometimes we have to think while we're singing. There are two ways to sing this verse — one sounds like:

*Glory to God all,
Glory in the highest*

Doesn't it sound better if you sing it like you'd say it?

*Glory to God,
All—Glory in the high—est*

So, remember — you're not singing to "God-all," but instead you're singing "Glory to God," [yes indeed!] "All glory in the highest!"

Week 1, Day 5
Born This Happy Morning

Simeon and Anna Recognize the Lord in Jesus, Rembrandt, 1627

**Yea, Lord, we greet Thee, born this happy morning;
Jesus, to Thee be all glory given;
Word of the Father, now in flesh appearing.**

What a happy day indeed that saw the promises fulfilled – a Savior born to a fallen world! This verse makes us think of Simeon and Anna in the temple, though they did not find out the Lord had come until the Babe was a few weeks old. Do you know their story?

Now there was a man in Jerusalem, whose name was Simeon, and this man was righteous and devout, waiting for the consolation of Israel, and the Holy Spirit was upon him. And it had been revealed to him by the Holy Spirit that he would not see death before he had seen the Lord's Christ. And he came in the Spirit into the temple, and when the parents brought in the child Jesus, to do for him according to the custom of the Law, he took him up in his arms and blessed God and said,

"Lord, now you are letting your servant depart in peace,
* according to your word;*
for my eyes have seen your salvation
that you have prepared in the presence of all peoples,
a light for revelation to the Gentiles,
* and for glory to your people Israel."*

And his father and his mother marveled at what was said about him. And Simeon blessed them and said to Mary his mother, "Behold, this child is appointed for the fall and rising of many in Israel, and for a sign that is opposed (and a sword will pierce through your own soul also), so that thoughts from many hearts may be revealed."

And there was a prophetess, Anna, the daughter of Phanuel, of the tribe of Asher. She was advanced in years, having lived with her husband seven years from when she was a virgin, and then as a widow until she was eighty-four. She did not depart from the temple, worshiping with fasting and prayer night and day. And coming up at that very hour she began to give thanks to God and to speak of him to all who were waiting for the redemption of Jerusalem. Luke 2:25-38

Simeon had been promised by the Spirit that He would not see death before he had seen the Messiah. Can you imagine that old man's joy in seeing the promises come true? And Anna, an elderly widow who shared the hope of the Savior with Temple-goers night and day, must have been overjoyed. It delights me to think of their expressions when they saw their Infant King!

As we have studied this week, Jesus, the King whose birth we celebrate at Christmas, is fully man, but also fully God. As God, He should be worshipped and given all glory. Jesus is the Word of God become flesh, a man, in order to take the punishment for our sins so that we could be reconciled to God. His birth is a joyous occasion, but we should remember that the joy comes from our Father God's love for us:

For God so loved the world that He gave His only begotten Son, that whoever believes in Him should not perish but have everlasting life. John 3:16

Let's not ever forget that! The joy of Christmas is our joy in God's tender love for us, that He sent His Son to live as one of us and to die in our place. Let's pray!

Week 2, Day 1
Hark, the Herald Angels Sing

From the *Bibel in Bildern*, Schnorr von Carolsfeld, 1860

This is one of those hymns that we think we all know, but people usually only sing the first verse. This is like nibbling on the salad and walking out on the feast. Charles Wesley packed so much Biblical truth into this carol, it's really worth the trouble to understand it all.

This week we're going to discuss the incarnation, the protoevangelium (That's a hard word, but as soon as we explain, it'll be really obvious to you!), Christ to the nations, the resurrection, and the Lord as the Second Adam. And it's all there in a carol we all love.

Hark! The herald angels sing,
"Glory to the newborn King;
Peace on earth, and mercy mild,
God and sinners reconciled!"
Joyful, all ye nations rise,
Join the triumph of the skies;
With th'angelic host proclaim,
"Christ is born in Bethlehem!"

In this verse, the very first word is one that needs explanation. "Hark" is a way of getting attention, like saying, "Hey!" or "Listen up!" If you also realize that a herald is someone that announces news, you'll see that the angels aren't flying about singing, "Hark! Hark!" Instead, the singer is calling to his friends "Hey, listen! The angels are singing!"

And what are they singing about? These were the angels that brought news to the shepherds and very important news it was: the Messiah who would bring reconciliation between God and man had been born. What do we mean by reconciliation? Well, do you remember a time that you disobeyed your parents and were punished? When you repented and asked forgiveness, your parents forgave you, didn't they? Your accounts were settled and justice had been done. Jesus came to take our punishment so we could be forgiven!

In this verse, the angels are shown giving glory to the newborn king. That little baby didn't stay an infant. One day, He will be recognized as the King of Kings, Revelation 19 tells us.

He is also seen in this verse as the One who will bring the nations to repentance, not only the Jews, but Gentiles, too.

"For my house shall be called a house of prayer
  for all nations." Isaiah 56:7

Arise, shine, for your light has come,
  and the glory of the Lord has risen upon you.
For behold, darkness shall cover the earth,
  and thick darkness the peoples;
but the Lord will arise upon you,
  and his glory will be seen upon you.

And nations shall come to your light,
  and kings to the brightness of your rising. Isaiah 60:1-3

Ever since we studied the history of Rome for the first time, we have grabbed onto the idea of a Triumph, a victory parade and celebration the Romans would give a conquering hero on his return to Rome, and we do this around the house whenever someone conquers something – a difficult situation, a textbook, some accomplishment. Isn't it encouraging to think about the triumph of the skies, the rejoicing of the angels in the birth of the Savior that would conquer death and sin?

[Listen to the tune in Midi format <u>at Hymnary</u> or learn more about the hymn.]

Hark the Herald Angels Sing!

This lovely hymn by Charles Wesley is more full of truth than many sermons and can imprint these precious truths on our hearts.
Felix Mendelssohn composed the melody in his cantata celebrating the 400th anniversary of Gutenberg's invention of the printing press.

Hark! The herald angels sing,
"Glory to the newborn King;
Peace on earth, and mercy mild,
God and sinners reconciled!"
Joyful, all ye nations rise,
Join the triumph of the skies;
With th'angelic host proclaim,
"Christ is born in Bethlehem!"

Refrain
Hark! the herald angels sing,
"Glory to the newborn King!"

Christ, by highest Heav'n adored;
Christ the everlasting Lord;
Late in time, behold Him come,
Offspring of a virgin's womb.
Veiled in flesh the Godhead see;
Hail th'incarnate Deity,
Pleased with us in flesh to dwell,
Jesus our Emmanuel.

Refrain

Hail the heav'nly Prince of Peace!
Hail the Sun of Righteousness!
Light and life to all He brings,
Ris'n with healing in His wings.
Mild He lays His glory by,
Born that man no more may die.
Born to raise the sons of earth,
Born to give them second birth.

Refrain

Come, Desire of nations, come,
Fix in us Thy humble home;
Rise, the woman's conqu'ring Seed,
Bruise in us the serpent's head.
Adam's likeness, Lord, efface,
Stamp Thine image in its place:
Second Adam from above,
Reinstate us in Thy love.

Refrain

Week 2, Day 2
Veiled in Flesh, the Godhead See

The Annunciation, El Greco, Prado, 1570

Usually, teaching the first stanza of familiar hymns means correcting misunderstandings about the language (like angels singing, "Hark!"). The second stanza is where you usually find the first totally new lyrics. It's where you often find new insights, too, since the words are fresh and we haven't grown complacent from hearing them a hundred times a week on the radio!

Christ, by highest Heav'n adored;
Christ the everlasting Lord;
Late in time, behold Him come,
Offspring of a virgin's womb.
Veiled in flesh the Godhead see;
Hail th'incarnate Deity,
Pleased as man with men to dwell,
Jesus our Emmanuel.

Verse two talks about the incarnation. Our Lord Jesus Christ is **not** merely a wonderful teacher, as some say, He is part of the Trinity, present at Creation, adored by the angels in heaven, and is eternal.

"Late in time, behold Him come," recalls that Jesus' birth was the completion of *thousands* of years of prophecy and expectation.

when the fulness of the time was come, God sent forth his Son, made of a woman ... Galations 4:4

"Offspring of a virgin's womb," means that Jesus was born to a virgin – a pure young woman who was not married. But babies need fathers, don't they? Yes! God is Jesus's father.

Therefore the Lord himself will give you a sign. Behold, the virgin shall conceive and bear a son, and shall call his name Immanuel. Isaiah 7:14

"Veiled in flesh, the Godhead see," reminds us that Jesus looked like any other man – his glory was veiled or hidden, but because He was God made flesh (remember John 1:1), we are able to see something of who God is and what holiness is like.

In "Hail the incarnate deity," hail means to praise or acclaim, "incarnate" means made of flesh, and the "deity" is God, so we praise the God in flesh, the God-man Jesus Christ.

What's really amazing is that God is pleased to do this for us! Even the name Emmanuel (or Immanuel) means "God with us."

All this took place to fulfill what the Lord had spoken by the prophet:
"Behold, the virgin shall conceive and bear a son, and they shall call his name Immanuel" (which means, God with us). Matthew 1:22-23

What riches of truth! Let's pray!

Week 2, Day 3
Born That Man No More May Die

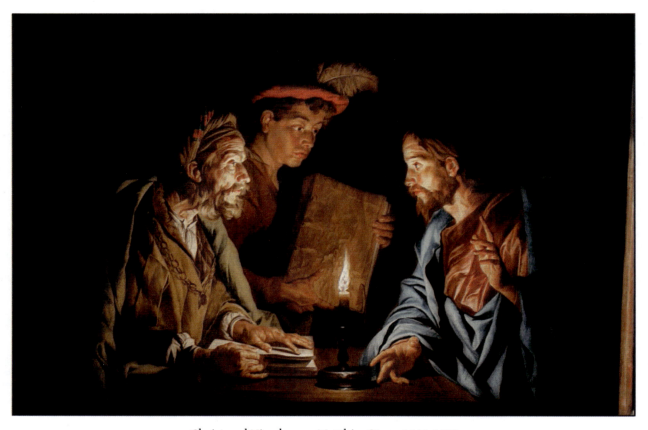

Christ and Nicodemus, Matthias Stom, 1640-1650

Hail the heav'nly Prince of Peace!
Hail the Sun of Righteousness!
Light and life to all He brings,
Ris'n with healing in His wings.
Mild He lays His glory by,
Born that man no more may die.
Born to raise the sons of earth,
Born to give them second birth.

In the third verse, we are once again called to praise the Messiah and Wesley directs us to Scripture after Scripture. "Hail the heavenly Prince of Peace," refers to this passage:

For to us a child is born,
  to us a son is given;
and the government shall be upon his shoulder,
  and his name shall be called
Wonderful Counselor, Mighty God,
  Everlasting Father, Prince of Peace. Isaiah 9:6

While "Hail the Sun of Righteousness," and "Risen with healing in His wings," refers to this one:

But for you who fear my name, the sun of righteousness shall rise with healing in its wings. You shall go out leaping like calves from the stall. Malachi 4:2

Philippians 2 gives us the clue to "Mild He lays his glory by," when it explains that Jesus hid his glory in taking on flesh like us:

...emptied himself, by taking the form of a servant, being born in the likeness of men. Philippians 2:7

The last part of the verse explains Christ's coming and our salvation. Jesus was indeed "Born to raise the sons of earth," that's you and me:

For I have come down from heaven, not to do my own will but the will of him who sent me. And this is the will of him who sent me, that I should lose nothing of all that he has given me, but raise it up on the last day. For this is the will of my Father, that everyone who looks on the Son and believes in him should have eternal life, and I will raise him up on the last day." John 6:38-40

What do you think, "Born to give them second birth," means? If you find that a little confusing, so did Nicodemus.

Now there was a man of the Pharisees named Nicodemus, a ruler of the Jews. This man came to Jesus by night and said to him, "Rabbi, we know that you are a teacher come from God, for no one can do these signs that you do unless God is with him." Jesus answered him, "Truly, truly, I say to you, unless one is born again he cannot see the kingdom of God." Nicodemus said to him, "How can a man be born when he is old? Can he enter a second time into his mother's womb and be born?" Jesus answered, "Truly, truly, I say to you, unless one is born of water and the Spirit, he cannot enter the kingdom of God. That which is born of the flesh is flesh, and that which is born of the Spirit is spirit. Do not marvel that I said to you, 'You must be born again.' The wind blows where it wishes, and you hear its sound, but you do not know where it comes from or where it goes. So it is with everyone who is born of the Spirit."

Nicodemus said to him, "How can these things be?" Jesus answered him, "Are you the teacher of Israel and yet you do not understand these things? Truly, truly, I say to you, we speak of what we know, and bear witness to what we have seen, but you do not receive our testimony. If I have told you earthly things and you do not believe, how can you believe if I tell you heavenly things? No one has ascended into heaven except he who descended from heaven, the Son of Man. And as Moses lifted up the serpent in the wilderness, so must the Son of Man be lifted up, that whoever believes in him may have eternal life. "For God so loved the world, that he gave his only Son, that whoever believes in him should not perish but have eternal life. John 3:1-16

The Lord explained to Nicodemus that our sin condemns us, but that if we believe in Him, we can be saved from the consequences of our sin and live forever with Him in heaven. When we do that, it's like being born a second time. Jesus came to give us a second birth. Do you understand that? Have you repented of your sin and trusted Jesus to save you?

Let's pray!

WEEK 2, DAY 4
COME, DESIRE OF NATIONS, COME

The Garden of Eden, Jan Brueghel the Elder, 1615

Come, Desire of nations, come,
Fix in us Thy humble home;
Rise, the woman's conqu'ring Seed,
Bruise in us the serpent's head.
Adam's likeness, Lord, efface,
Stamp Thine image in its place:
Second Adam from above,
Reinstate us in Thy love.

The fourth verse and last verse that we sing uses the first four lines of each of the last two verses Charles Wesley wrote, but it works together incredibly well.

This verse addresses the *protoevangelium*. That's a very big word, but it just means the early or first gospel, when our dear Father gave Adam and Eve hope for the Savior to come. "Rise, the woman's conquering Seed, Bruise in us the serpent's head," points us to Genesis 3, speaking to the serpent, Satan, God said,

And I will put enmity Between you and the woman, And between your seed and her Seed; He shall bruise your head, And you shall bruise His heel. Genesis 3:15

"Rise, the woman's conquering Seed," the carol tells us. It was finally time for the Savior who was promised at the beginning of the world to come and restore us to fellowship with God and renew our nature, which was ruined in the Fall. His coming and dying paid the penalty for the sins of God's people so that they could be reconciled to God.

And He is coming for all of His people, more than just the children of Abraham, but His people in every nation, too! He is what we are longing for, "Come, Desire of Nations, Come."

"For thus says the Lord of hosts: 'Once more (it is a little while) I will shake heaven and earth, the sea and dry land; and I will shake all nations, and they shall come to the Desire of All Nations, and I will fill this temple with glory,' says the Lord of hosts." Haggai 2:6-7

The last part of the verse teaches us about Christ as the second Adam, "Second Adam from above, reinstate us in Thy love."

For since by man came death, by Man also came the resurrection of the dead. For as in Adam all die, even so in Christ all shall be made alive. I Corinthians 15:22

Because Adam, the first man, sinned, we have all inherited a sin nature and we are all separated from God.

For as by one man's disobedience many were made sinners, so also by one Man's obedience many will be made righteous. Roman 5:19, though the whole passage from verse 12 is very worth reading.

Another reference to the Lord as the second Adam is in I Corinthians.

And so it is written, "The first man Adam became a living being." The last Adam became a life-giving spirit. I Corinthians 15:45

But, what is meant by, "Adam's likeness, Lord, efface, Stamp Thine image in its place?" Efface means to wipe out.

Do not lie to one another, since you have put off the old man with his deeds, and have put on the new man who is renewed in knowledge according to the image of Him who created him..." Colossians 3:9-10

This passage explains that we have to put off the old man and put on the new.

For whom He foreknew, He also predestined to be conformed to the image of His Son, that He might be the firstborn among many brethren. Moreover whom He predestined, these

He also called; whom He called, these He also justified; and whom He justified, these He also glorified. Romans 8:29-30

We should be conformed to the image of Christ, which is why the hymn says "stamp Thine image in its place."

This last verse reminds us that the Lord Jesus Christ's birth (and death) is the culmination of thousands of years of prophecies beginning in the Garden of Eden. There is incredible theological and devotional richness in this Christmas hymn.

Let's pray!

Week 2, Day 5
A Day of Mercy

Sometimes, we don't accomplish all that we want to. Occasionally, we're providentially hindered. That means the Lord brings other things into our lives and we're prevented from doing what we planned. More often, we fail to plan well or lack the self-control to carry through our plans.

Did you know, though, that God still looks on those of us who believe with love and mercy? We do not have to somehow earn God's favor, which is a good thing, since Scripture says in Isaiah 64:6 that our righteousness is like filthy rags. Instead, God has imputed Christ's righteous to us:

...and be found in Him, not having my own righteousness, which is from the law, but that which is through faith in Christ, the righteousness which is from God by faith...
Philippians 3:9

So, if you've missed a day and you are behind, this is your catch-up day. If you haven't, you can have a day of carol singing! Be sure to sing all the verses of the ones we've studied, but sing some more, too.

Enjoy!

Week 3, Day 1
We Three Kings of Orient Are

Caspar, Jan van Bijlert, 1640–1650

"We Three Kings" is one of those songs that seems pretty lightweight and simple. That is, until you sing more than the first verse! There's actually a world of meaning in this hymn. Let's start with the first verse:

We three kings of Orient are;
Bearing gifts we traverse afar,
Field and fountain, moor and mountain,
Following yonder star.

Refrain
O star of wonder, star of light,
Star with royal beauty bright,
Westward leading, still proceeding,
Guide us to thy perfect light.

"We three kings of Orient are," is referring to the Wise Men who came to worship the Christ child. Did you know that we don't actually know how many of them there were or even if they were kings? Legend has it that they were kings and that their names were Caspar, Melchior, and Balthazar of India, Persia, and Babylonia or Arabia, respectively. That's why German carolers chalk something like "20 C+M+B 20" on the lintels of homes they visit. The numbers refer to the year and the letters to both the initials of the Wise Men and *Christus mansionem benedicat*, Latin for "Christ bless this home."

The Word of God doesn't give us that kind of detail, though! What *do* we know?

Now after Jesus was born in Bethlehem of Judea in the days of Herod the king, behold, wise men from the east came to Jerusalem, saying, "Where is he who has been born king of the Jews? For we saw his star when it rose and have come to worship him." When Herod the king heard this, he was troubled, and all Jerusalem with him; and assembling all the chief priests and scribes of the people, he inquired of them where the Christ was to be born. They told him, "In Bethlehem of Judea, for so it is written by the prophet:

"'And you, O Bethlehem, in the land of Judah,
   are by no means least among the rulers of Judah;
for from you shall come a ruler
   who will shepherd my people Israel.'"

Then Herod summoned the wise men secretly and ascertained from them what time the star had appeared. And he sent them to Bethlehem, saying, "Go and search diligently for the child, and when you have found him, bring me word, that I too may come and worship him." After listening to the king, they went on their way. And behold, the star that they had seen when it rose went before them until it came to rest over the place where the child was. When they saw the star, they rejoiced exceedingly with great joy. And going into the house, they saw the child with Mary his mother, and they fell down and worshiped him. Then, opening their treasures, they offered him gifts, gold and frankincense and myrrh. And being warned in a dream not to return to Herod, they departed to their own country by another way. Matthew 2:1-12

The word translated as wise men is magi, which refers to Persian priests who have made a study of the stars. Where did people get the idea that they were kings, then? They looked at passages like these:

Because of your temple at Jerusalem
   kings shall bear gifts to you. Psalm 68:29 and

May the kings of Tarshish and of the coastlands
  render him tribute;
may the kings of Sheba and Seba
  bring gifts!
May all kings fall down before him,
  all nations serve him! Psalm 72:10-11

The truth of the matter is that we can't really be sure whether these passages are talking about the Wise Men or about kings in future generations. It's possible that the legends that have been passed down are accurate, but we certainly can't be sure.

What we can be sure about is that God graciously led these wise men of pagan nations to find out about the birth of Jesus Christ and led them to find the young child, probably not the night of the birth, since the passage says they found Him in a house, but to find Him nonetheless, and bring him gifts and worship him!

In the past, this event was celebrated on January 6th and was called Epiphany. It' was considered the end of the Christmas season, when the Twelve Days of Christmas were complete. It's a day when gifts were exchanged, remembering the gifts of the Magi and also the greatest gift of all, salvation through Jesus Christ.

God has been even more gracious to us than to the Wise Men. We don't have to figure out from stars and legend where the King is, we are told all about Him in the Word of God. That is a great blessing.

Let's pray!

[Play a midi file with the tune at Hymnary where you can also read more about it.]

WE THREE KINGS

If you only sing the first verse and refrain you miss the awesome message that Christ came to die for us! It was written by John H. Hopkins, Jr. for a Christmas pageant at General Theological Seminary in New York City in 1857.

We three kings of Orient are;
Bearing gifts we traverse afar,
Field and fountain, moor and mountain,
Following yonder star.

Refrain
O star of wonder, star of light,
Star with royal beauty bright,
Westward leading, still proceeding,
Guide us to thy perfect light.

Born a King on Bethlehem's plain
Gold I bring to crown Him again,
King forever, ceasing never,
Over us all to reign.

Refrain

Frankincense to offer have I;
Incense owns a Deity nigh;
Prayer and praising, voices raising,
Worshipping God on high.

Refrain

Myrrh is mine, its bitter perfume
Breathes a life of gathering gloom;
Sorrowing, sighing, bleeding, dying,
Sealed in the stone cold tomb.

Refrain

Glorious now behold Him arise;
King and God and sacrifice;
Alleluia, Alleluia,
Sounds through the earth and skies.

Refrain

Week 3, Day 2
Born a King on Bethlehem's Plain

Christ Pantocrator, Russia, early 19th century

Born a King on Bethlehem's plain
Gold I bring to crown Him again,
King forever, ceasing never,
Over us all to reign.

This verse takes the gift of gold that the Wise Men brought to Jesus and imagines why it was brought. Gold, a rare and valuable mineral, was reserved for very special purposes, such as the crowns that royalty wore. As we learned earlier this month, Revelation 19:11-16 tells us that Jesus is the King of all Kings. Listen to this passage that talks about the end of the ages:

Then I saw heaven opened, and behold, a white horse! The one sitting on it is called Faithful and True, and in righteousness he judges and makes war. His eyes are like a flame of fire, and on his head are many diadems, and he has a name written that no one knows but himself. He is clothed in a robe dipped in blood, and the name by which he is called is The Word of God. And the armies of heaven, arrayed in fine linen, white and pure, were following him on white horses. From his mouth comes a sharp sword with which to strike down the nations, and he will rule them with a rod of iron. He will tread the winepress of the fury of the wrath of God the Almighty. On his robe and on his thigh he has a name written, King of kings and Lord of lords. Revelation 19:11-16

Why does it say, "Gold I bring to crown him again," – why does it say *again*? Jesus is not King because humans will one day recognize Him as King, He is King because He has always been King. He is Creator God, the one who has made us all, even kings.

He was the one that the prophet Micah declared would be born in Bethlehem in Micah 5:2. And He is the one that John the Apostle wrote about in Revelation,

Then the seventh angel blew his trumpet, and there were loud voices in heaven, saying, "The kingdom of the world has become the kingdom of our Lord and of his Christ, and he shall reign forever and ever." Revelation 11:15

As we look at the world around us, it's encouraging to think that one day we will all be under the reign of Christ.

Week 3, Day 3
Worshipping God on High

Adoration of the Magi, Rafael, 1502-1504

Frankincense to offer have I;
Incense owns a Deity nigh;
Prayer and praising, voices raising,
Worshipping God on high.

"Frankincense to offer have I," and the second gift the Word mentions that the Magi brought was frankincense. Frankincense is the aromatic resin of the Boswellia tree and was thought to be very difficult to harvest according to the ancient writer Herodotus. It was also the base ingredient in the incense that God told the Israelites to burn in the Tabernacle.

The Lord said to Moses, "Take sweet spices, stacte, and onycha, and galbanum, sweet spices with pure frankincense (of each shall there be an equal part), and make an incense blended as by the perfumer, seasoned with salt, pure and holy. You shall beat some of it very small, and put part of it before the testimony in the tent of meeting where I shall meet with you. It shall be most holy for you. And the incense that you shall make according to its composition, you shall not make for yourselves. It shall be for you holy to the Lord. Whoever makes any like it to use as perfume shall be cut off from his people." Exodus 30:34-38

As you can see, this incense was reserved for the worship of God alone. That makes frankincense a very significant gift, doesn't it?

"Incense owns a diety nigh," or, this incense means that God is nearby, points out that frankincense was a very appropriate thing to bring the Babe that was the God-man, Jesus Christ, because He is deity, another word for God.

See to it that no one takes you captive by philosophy and empty deceit, according to human tradition, according to the elemental spirits of the world, and not according to Christ. For in him the whole fullness of deity dwells bodily, and you have been filled in him, who is the head of all rule and authority. Colossians 2:8-10

That's pretty plain when it says, "the whole fullness of deity dwells bodily." Jesus is fully God and He deserves our worship.

"Prayer and praising, voices raising, Worshipping God on high," encourages us to do just that. Psalm 100 gives us a pattern for worship, praising God in song and prayer.

Make a joyful shout to the Lord, all you lands!
Serve the Lord with gladness;
Come before His presence with singing.
Know that the Lord, He is God;
It is He who has made us, and not we ourselves;
We are His people and the sheep of His pasture.

Enter into His gates with thanksgiving,
And into His courts with praise.
Be thankful to Him, and bless His name.
For the Lord is good;
His mercy is everlasting,
And His truth endures to all generations. Psalm 100

This is a wonderful time of year to make those joyful shouts and to serve the Lord with gladness because He loved us so much that He sent His son to save us!

Let's pray!

WEEK 3, DAY 4
SEALED IN THE STONE COLD TOMB

Crucifixion of Jesus, woodcut, Gustave Dore, 1866

Myrrh is mine, its bitter perfume
Breathes a life of gathering gloom;
Sorrowing, sighing, bleeding, dying,
Sealed in the stone cold tomb.

The third and last of the gifts mentioned in Scripture is myrrh, "Myrrh is mine, its bitter perfume." Myrrh is the resin or gum of a number of small, thorny trees, which are repeatedly wounded so that secret the gum. The name myrrh comes from a Hebrew word which means bitter and later, when the word made its way into Greek, meant perfume in general.

Myrrh is mentioned several times in Scripture. In Genesis, Joseph's brothers sold him to

...a caravan of Ishmaelites coming from Gilead, with their camels bearing gum, balm, and myrrh, on their way to carry it down to Egypt. Genesis 37:25-28

It was used as part of the holy anointing oil in the Tabernacle:

The Lord said to Moses, "Take the finest spices: of liquid myrrh 500 shekels, and of sweet-smelling cinnamon half as much, that is, 250, and 250 of aromatic cane, and 500 of cassia, according to the shekel of the sanctuary, and a hin of olive oil. And you shall make of these a sacred anointing oil blended as by the perfumer; it shall be a holy anointing oil. Exodus 30:22-25

Myrrh was used as an analgesic, or painkiller, and it was offered to Jesus at the crucifixion, but he did not take it.

And they brought him to the place called Golgotha (which means Place of a Skull). And they offered him wine mixed with myrrh, but he did not take it. And they crucified him and divided his garments among them, casting lots for them, to decide what each should take. Mark 11:22-24

Finally, it was used to prepare bodies for burial and was actually used to prepare the body of our Lord.

After these things Joseph of Arimathea, who was a disciple of Jesus, but secretly for fear of the Jews, asked Pilate that he might take away the body of Jesus, and Pilate gave him permission. So he came and took away his body. Nicodemus also, who earlier had come to Jesus by night, came bringing a mixture of myrrh and aloes, about seventy-five pounds in weight. So they took the body of Jesus and bound it in linen cloths with the spices, as is the burial custom of the Jews. Now in the place where he was crucified there was a garden, and in the garden a new tomb in which no one had yet been laid. So because of the Jewish day of Preparation, since the tomb was close at hand, they laid Jesus there. John 19:38-42

That seems like a very oddly grim and depressing gift to give a baby, doesn't it? It makes sense, though, when we remember that the whole purpose of the birth of that Child was so that He could one day lay down His life as a sacrifice for our sins.

This verse is sung slowly, with sadness, as we remember what our salvation cost the Lord Jesus.

Let's pray!

Week 3, Day 5
Glorious Now Behold Him Arise

St John and St Peter at the Empty Tomb of Christ, Giovanni Francesco Romanelli, 1641

Glorious now behold Him arise;
King and God and sacrifice;
Alleluia, Alleluia,
Sounds through the earth and skies.

When you reach this verse, raise your voice and sing with joy! The sealed cold tomb is not the end of the story. Yes, Christ died as a sacrifice for our sin. The third day, though, He rose from the dead as a sign that God the Father accepted His sacrifice.

But on the first day of the week, at early dawn, they went to the tomb, taking the spices they had prepared. And they found the stone rolled away from the tomb, but when they went in they did not find the body of the Lord Jesus. While they were perplexed about this, behold, two men stood by them in dazzling apparel. And as they were frightened and bowed their faces to the ground, the men said to them, "Why do you seek the living among the dead? He is not here, but has risen. Remember how he told you, while he was still in Galilee, that the Son of Man must be delivered into the hands of sinful men and be crucified and on the third day rise." And they remembered his words, and returning from the tomb they told all these things to the eleven and to all the rest. Luke 24:1-9

Because Jesus rose from the dead, we know that those of us who believe will be raised again one day, too!

But we do not want you to be uninformed, brothers, about those who are asleep, that you may not grieve as others do who have no hope. For since we believe that Jesus died and rose again, even so, through Jesus, God will bring with him those who have fallen asleep. For this we declare to you by a word from the Lord, that we who are alive, who are left until the coming of the Lord, will not precede those who have fallen asleep. For the Lord himself will descend from heaven with a cry of command, with the voice of an archangel, and with the sound of the trumpet of God. And the dead in Christ will rise first. Then we who are alive, who are left, will be caught up together with them in the clouds to meet the Lord in the air, and so we will always be with the Lord. Therefore encourage one another with these words. I Thessalonians 4:13-18

That is really good news!

"King and God and sacrifice" refers back to the last three verses, which describe how Jesus is King of Kings, how He is truly God and truly man, and how He is the perfect sacrifice for our sins.

"Alleluia, Alleluia, Sounds through the earth and skies," is a resounding praise to God. Alleluia, also spelled hallulujah, means "God be praised," but it has the sense of loud, joyful worship, like a shout of praise!

Jesus, our King and God and sacrifice, is truly worthy of all of our praise! That's why we're learning these songs.

Let's pray!

Week 4, Day 1
Angels from the Realms of Glory

The Angel Appearing to the Shepherds, Rembrandt, 1634

One of our favorite Christmas carols is Angels from the Realms of Glory. Notice how wonderfully it tells of the reactions of the different witnesses to the Messiah's coming: the angels, the shepherds, the wise men, even Anna and Simeon in the Temple. It's the entire Christmas story in one song and it's a great way to review all that we've studied during Advent.

Let's talk about the first two verses. These verses set the stage of the Annunciation to the Shepherds, or the angels' announcement to the shepherds.

Angels from the realms of glory,
Wing your flight o'er all the earth;
Ye who sang creation's story
Now proclaim Messiah's birth.

Shepherds, in the field abiding,
Watching o'er your flocks by night,
God with us is now residing;
Yonder shines the infant light:

Angels in Scripture are very different from the cherubs we sometimes see in classical paintings. Instead, they are mighty, glorious creatures, whose usually have to tell people, "Fear not!" when they appear to them!

"Angels from the realms of glory, wing your flight over all the earth," pictures that incredible moment when the heavens opened and the multitude of the heavenly host appeared to the shepherds. The realms of glory is referring to heaven.

"Ye who sang creation's story" points to a passage that may not be familiar to you. In the book of Job, Job had been sorely tested by trials. Both he and his friends (Who blamed him, that's why we refer to people who aren't much help as Job's Comforters) sought to figure out why in the world he had suffered so much. Finally, God answered and reminded them all they He was God and they were not.

"Where were you when I laid the foundation of the earth?
Tell me, if you have understanding.
Who determined its measurements—surely you know!
Or who stretched the line upon it?
On what were its bases sunk,
or who laid its cornerstone,
when the morning stars sang together
and all the sons of God shouted for joy? Job 38:4-7

We know that the sons of God in Job refers to the angels from a mention in Job 1:6, so we see here that they were present at the creation of the Earth and sang praises to God, just like it says in this verse!

"Now proclaim Messiah's birth," is the next line. The Hebrew word that we pronounce messiah means "Anointed One," the same meaning as the Greek word *khristos*, which we call Christ. The angels are announcing the birth of the one that would fulfill the hundreds of Messianic prophecies in the Old Testament. This passage was written over five hundred years before the birth of Christ:

"Rejoice greatly, O daughter of Zion!
Shout, O daughter of Jerusalem!
Behold, your King is coming to you;
He is just and having salvation,
Lowly and riding on a donkey,
A colt, the foal of a donkey. Zechariah 9:9

Do you recognize the fulfillment of that prophecy? How about the Triumphal Entry on Palm Sunday recorded in John 12:12-16 and in the other gospels, as well.

In the second verse, "Shepherds, in the field abiding, Watching o'er your flocks by night," the attention shifts to the shepherds out in the countryside.

"God with us is now residing; Yonder shines the infant light:" is the crux of the angels' announcement. The greatest miracle yet has occurred – God has taken on flesh and is living with His people. We call this the incarnation.

How did the shepherds respond?

So it was, when the angels had gone away from them into heaven, that the shepherds said to one another, "Let us now go to Bethlehem and see this thing that has come to pass, which the Lord has made known to us." And they came with haste and found Mary and Joseph, and the Babe lying in a manger. Now when they had seen Him, they made widely known the saying which was told them concerning this Child. And all those who heard it marveled at those things which were told them by the shepherds. But Mary kept all these things and pondered them in her heart. Then the shepherds returned, glorifying and praising God for all the things that they had heard and seen, as it was told them. Luke 2:15-20

That's a pretty good example for us to follow – to make "widely known the saying which was told them" and "glorifying and praising God for all the things that they had heard and seen." Let's be like the shepherds.

[You can listen to a Midi file of the tune at Hymnary and learn more about the carol, too!]

Let's pray!

Angels from the Realms of Glory

The whole Christmas story in a song!

Angels from the realms of glory,
Wing your flight o'er all the earth;
Ye who sang creation's story
Now proclaim Messiah's birth.

Refrain

Come and worship,
Come and worship,
Worship Christ, the newborn King.

Shepherds, in the field abiding,
Watching o'er your flocks by night,
God with us is now residing;
Yonder shines the infant light:

Refrain

Sages, leave your contemplations,
Brighter visions beam afar;
Seek the great Desire of nations;
Ye have seen His natal star.

Refrain

Saints, before the altar bending,
Watching long in hope and fear;
Suddenly the Lord, descending,
In His temple shall appear.

Refrain

Sinners, wrung with true repentance,
Doomed for guilt to endless pains,
Justice now revokes the sentence,
Mercy calls you; break your chains.

Refrain

Though an Infant now we view Him,
He shall fill His Father's throne,
Gather all the nations to Him;
Every knee shall then bow down:

Refrain

All creation, join in praising
God, the Father, Spirit, Son,
Evermore your voices raising
To th'eternal Three in One.

Refrain

Week 4, Day 2
Brighter Visions Beam Afar

The Adoration of the Magi, Albrecht Durer, 1504

Sages, leave your contemplations,
Brighter visions beam afar;
Seek the great Desire of nations;
Ye have seen His natal star.

Come and worship,
Come and worship,
Worship Christ the newborn King

The verses of "Angels from the Realms of Glory" call out to different groups of people and call them to worship. In this verse, the carol calls out to the Wise Men.

"Sages leave your contemplations," it says. Sage is another word for the wise. Someone is considered a sage when his wisdom is recognized by all. The verse encourages the Magi to leave their deep thoughts and studies, their contemplations, because "Brighter visions beam afar." There is something more wonderful than anything they could find in their studies of the stars, research in science, or philosophical musings. Real wisdom would be found at the end of their journey.

Give instruction to a wise man, and he will be still wiser;
Teach a just man, and he will increase in learning.
"The fear of the Lord is the beginning of wisdom,
And the knowledge of the Holy One is understanding. Proverbs 9:9-10

"Seek the great Desire of nations; Ye have seen His natal star." The Wise Men were the first of the nations, the non-Jews, who would worship at the feet of Jesus. What an amazing thing that the gospel would reach beyond the Chosen People to the nations who had been in rebellion against God for millennia.

"I was watching in the night visions,
And behold, One like the Son of Man,
Coming with the clouds of heaven!
He came to the Ancient of Days,
And they brought Him near before Him.
Then to Him was given dominion and glory and a kingdom,
That all peoples, nations, and languages should serve Him.
His dominion is an everlasting dominion,
Which shall not pass away,
And His kingdom the one
Which shall not be destroyed. Daniel 7:13-14

Have you ever thought about that? For several years now, Keith and Kristyn Getty, Christian singers and songwriters have hosted an international singalong, encouraging congregations to send in recordings. It isamazing to hear God's praises in so many languages sung by people of so many nations. It's like a little taste of heaven. You can listen and watch <u>online.</u>

Like the sages in this verse, we need to realize that real wisdom is in the Word of God and that one day we will be able to worship with people from every people group on earth.

Let's pray!

WEEK 4, DAY 3
Watching Long in Hope and Fear

Simeon and Anna Praise the Infant Jesus, Arent de Gelder, c.1700

Saints, before the altar bending,
Watching long in hope and fear;
Suddenly the Lord, descending,
In His temple shall appear.

Come and worship,
Come and worship,
Worship Christ, the newborn King.

Who are the "Saints, before the altar bending, watching long in hope and fear?"
In the Christmas story, they're Anna and Simeon, as we heard earlier this month.

In the larger scope of things, though, this verse reminds us that Jesus' birth and life had been the subject of hundreds of prophecies. Servants of God had been studying those prophecies and longing for the coming of the Messiah since God gave us the very first prophecy about Jesus in the Garden of Eden! Saints, or those sanctified and purified by God, refers to all those who believed in the Savior to come.

Let's look at some of those prophecies in one of the richest passages that describes the coming Lord. Notice the detail here – about His mission to save us and about the details of His suffering and death.

Who has believed our report?
And to whom has the arm of the Lord been revealed?
For He shall grow up before Him as a tender plant,
And as a root out of dry ground.
He has no form or comeliness;
And when we see Him,
There is no beauty that we should desire Him.
He is despised and rejected by men,
A Man of sorrows and acquainted with grief.
And we hid, as it were, our faces from Him;
He was despised, and we did not esteem Him.

Surely He has borne our griefs
And carried our sorrows;
Yet we esteemed Him stricken,
Smitten by God, and afflicted.
But He was wounded for our transgressions,
He was bruised for our iniquities;
The chastisement for our peace was upon Him,
And by His stripes we are healed.
All we like sheep have gone astray;
We have turned, every one, to his own way;
And the Lord has laid on Him the iniquity of us all.

He was oppressed and He was afflicted,
Yet He opened not His mouth;
He was led as a lamb to the slaughter,
And as a sheep before its shearers is silent,
So He opened not His mouth.
He was taken from prison and from judgment,
And who will declare His generation?

For He was cut off from the land of the living;
For the transgressions of My people He was stricken.
And they made His grave with the wicked—
But with the rich at His death,
Because He had done no violence,
Nor was any deceit in His mouth.

Yet it pleased the Lord to bruise Him;
He has put Him to grief.
When You make His soul an offering for sin,
He shall see His seed, He shall prolong His days,
And the pleasure of the Lord shall prosper in His hand.
He shall see the labor of His soul, and be satisfied.
By His knowledge My righteous Servant shall justify many,
For He shall bear their iniquities.
Therefore I will divide Him a portion with the great,
And He shall divide the spoil with the strong,
Because He poured out His soul unto death,
And He was numbered with the transgressors,
And He bore the sin of many,
And made intercession for the transgressors. Isaiah 53

If you have time, you might read over some of the other prophecies that were exactly fulfilled in the life of Christ:

Psalm 22:16-18 – His hands and feets would be pierced, his bones unbroken, and they would cast lots for his garments.

Zechariah 11:12-13 – He would be betrayed for thirty pieces of silver which would buy the Potter's Field.

Psalm 16:10 – He would be resurrected.

There are many, many more, too. Fulfilled prophecy is strong evidence for the reliability of Scripture. Only God could have known all these things so long before they happened. Scripture is God-breathed, or inspired, as Timothy tells us, and can be trusted.

All Scripture is given by inspiration of God, and is profitable for doctrine, for reproof, for correction, for instruction in righteousness, that the man of God may be complete, thoroughly equipped for every good work. II Timothy 3:16-17

Let's pray!

Week 4, Day 4
Mercy Calls You

The Liberation of St. Peter, Sebastiano Ricci, 1722

**Sinners, wrung with true repentance,
Doomed for guilt to endless pains,
Justice now revokes the sentence,
Mercy calls you; break your chains.**

**Come and worship,
Come and worship,
Worship Christ, the newborn King.**

Now, the carol turns to us! This verse calls out to all hearers who realize their need of a Savior.

"Sinners…doomed for guilt to endless pain." Our sin separates us from God and condemns us to death and eternal punishment.

But your iniquities have separated you from your God;
And your sins have hidden His face from you,
So that He will not hear. Isaiah 59:2

If we say we have no sin, we deceive ourselves, and the truth is not in us. I John 1:8

Or do you not know that the unrighteous will not inherit the kingdom of God? I Corinthians 6:9

But as for the cowardly, the faithless, the detestable, as for murderers, the sexually immoral, sorcerers, idolaters, and all liars, their portion will be in the lake that burns with fire and sulfur, which is the second death." Revelation 21:8

That sad truth is not the end of the story, though!

"Sinners, wrung with true repentance…Justice now revokes the sentence, Mercy calls you; break your chains." God is so good! When we repent of our sins (That means to hate and forsake our sin, as displeasing to God, as the *Catechism for Boys and Girls* says.) and trust in Jesus's sacrifice to save us, our punishment is revoked!

"Repent therefore and be converted, that your sins may be blotted out…" Acts 3:19a

For by grace you have been saved through faith, and that not of yourselves; it is the gift of God, not of works, lest anyone should boast. Ephesians 2:8

Because, if you confess with your mouth that Jesus is Lord and believe in your heart that God raised him from the dead, you will be saved. Romans 10:9

What wonderful news! That's what the word gospel means, good news. God has promised to save all who trust in Jesus so that we are no longer slaves to sin.

"Come now, and let us reason together," Says the Lord,
"Though your sins are like scarlet, They shall be as white as snow;
Though they are red like crimson, They shall be as wool. Isaiah 1:18

If you haven't repented of your sin and trusted Jesus to save you, you can do that now.

Let's pray!

Week 4, Day 5
All Creation, Join in Praising

The Nativity, Caravaggio, 1609

**Though an Infant now we view Him,
He shall fill His Father's throne,
Gather all the nations to Him;
Every knee shall then bow down:**

**All creation, join in praising
God, the Father, Spirit, Son,
Evermore your voices raising
To th'eternal Three in One.**

The final verses of "Angels from the Realms of Glory" draw the attention of all the world to the One who deserves our worship.

"Though an Infant now we view Him, He shall fill His Father's throne," reminds us not to take the Baby Jesus lightly.

Behold, the virgin shall conceive and bear a Son, and shall call His name Immanuel … (Isaiah 7:14) … which is translated, "God with us." (Matthew 1:23)

Jesus Christ was born; He was not an average man who suddenly received a commission from God or a special revelation. As the angels told the shepherds, *"There is born to you this day in the city of David a Savior, who is Christ the Lord."* (Luke 2:11) Jesus appeared in human history in human form as a human **Infant**.

But God also said the coming Savior would fulfill His promise to King David, that there would be One to occupy David's throne forever. Isaiah 9 continues,

Of the increase of His government and peace,
There will be no end.
Upon the throne of David and over his kingdom
To order and establish it … forever (Isaiah 9:7)

For thus says the LORD: 'David shall never lack a man to sit on the throne of the house of Israel;' (Jeremiah 33:17)

So when the angel spoke to Mary, he told her that Jesus *"will be great, and will be called the Son of the Highest; and the Lord God will give Him the throne of His father David."* (Luke 1:32) And both Luke and Matthew explain how Jesus' earthly family was descended from King David, just to be sure. (Matthew 1:1-16, Luke 3:23-38) Jesus was the promised one to **fill His father's throne** – the throne of David.

"Gather all the nations to Him; Every knee shall then bow down…"

The Gospel is for all the world, not just David's kingdom. When the Bible speaks of "the nations," usually it means "the Gentile world." God promised special attention and blessings on the Israelites but told them His coming Savior would **gather the nations**, too.

Indeed, He [God] says,
"It is too small a thing You should be My Servant
To raise up the tribes of Jacob,
And to restore the preserved ones of Israel;

I will also give You as a light to the Gentiles,
That You should be My salvation to the ends of the earth." (Isaiah 49:6)

And now, we look forward to a day when all the earth will honor and worship Jesus their King – because

God also has highly exalted Him and given Him the name which is above every name, that at the name of Jesus **every knee should bow** *... and that every tongue should confess that Jesus Christ is Lord ...* (Philippians 2:9-11)

"All creation, join in praising God, the Father, Spirit, Son, Evermore your voices raising To th'eternal Three in One."

Jesus said if His disciples fall silent, *"the very stones would cry out."* (Luke 19:40 ESV) But the day will come when all of creation will rejoice over Him:

Let the sea roar, and all its fullness,
The world and those who dwell in it;
Let the rivers clap their hands;
Let the hills be joyful together before the LORD,
For He is coming to judge the earth.
With righteousness He shall judge the world,
And the peoples with equity. (Psalm 98:7-9)

This last stanza speaks of the mystery of the Trinity, God the Father, Christ the Son, and the Holy Spirit. The act of creation itself shows the work of all three:

In the beginning God created the heavens and the earth ... And the Spirit of God was hovering over the face of the waters. (Genesis 1:1-2)

In the beginning was the Word, and Word was with God, and the Word was God. ... All things were made through Him, and without Him nothing was made that was made. ... And the Word became flesh and dwelt among us, and we beheld His glory, the glory as of the only begotten of the Father, full of grace and truth. (John 1:1,3,14)

The Bible shows us in these passages and many others that the Father, the Son, and the Holy Spirit are all truly God, existing side by side in eternity. And all of creation speaks of God's glory:

Praise the LORD from the heavens;

Praise Him in the heights!
Praise Him, all His angels;
Praise Him, all His hosts!
Praise Him, sun and moon;
Praise Him, all you stars of light!
Praise Him, you heavens of heavens,
And you waters above the heavens!
Let them praise the name of the LORD,
For He commanded and they were created. (Psalm 148:1-5)

"Come and worship, Come and worship, Worship Christ, the newborn King," the carol calls to us. Let's do! This Christmas, let's remember and remind those around us that the celebration is not about us; it's about Jesus.

The gifts are a picture that God gave us the greatest gift of all.

The evergreens remind us that we have eternal life through Christ.

The red ribbons point to the blood that was shed for our sins.

The round wreaths have no beginning and no end, like our eternal God.

The gold ribbons and decorations remind us that this is the birth of a king.

The feast is a dim picture of that great feast we'll share in heaven – the Marriage Supper of the Lamb.

We have so much reason to be rejoice.

MERRY CHRISTMAS!

More Resources

Dear Friends,

We hope you've enjoyed using Christ-Centered Advent with your family! We have other resources that we hope you'll find helpful in making biblical family life practical in your home.

At RaisingRealMen.com find:

> Award-winning books on parenting and family life, like Raising Real Men, No Longer Little (for parents of tweens/preteens), and Love, Honor, and Virtue (for teen boys).
>
> Character-building audiobooks the whole family will enjoy.
>
> Gifts and gear your kids will love to receive and you can feel happy about buying.
>
> Educational resources, help for struggling and gifted learners.

Check out Craftsman Crate – the subscription box that builds your skills – for complete kits, real tools, and artisanal craft skills you can use the rest of your life.

Listen to our podcast, Making Biblical Family Life Practical, at HalandMelanie.com/radio or wherever you listen to podcasts.

Find out about inviting us to speak at HalandMelanie.com.

May the Lord bless you as you raise your children in the faith!

Your friends,

Hal & Melanie

Made in the USA
Middletown, DE
03 December 2023